THE WHY OF SPORTS
FINDING MEANING, PRESENCE AND PURPOSE IN THE GAME AND BEYOND

PETER BIDSTRUP

ISBN 979-8-9937273-0-1

For Brett, Larsen, and all my teammates in life

In the end, it's extra effort that separates a winner from second place. But winning takes a lot more than that, too. It starts with complete command of the fundamentals. Then it takes desire, determination, discipline, and self-sacrifice. And finally, it takes a great deal of love, fairness, and respect for your fellow man. Put all these together, and even if you don't win, how can you lose?

— Jesse Owens

Contents

PART TWO
THE INNER GAME: MASTERING ATTENTION, THOUGHTS, EMOTIONS, AND PRESENCE

PART FOUR
CONNECTION, COLLABORATION, AND LEADERSHIP: EXPANDING MASTERY BEYOND THE SELF

INTRODUCTION

My childhood revolved around two main pursuits: playing sports and exploring the natural world. My dad was a life-long teacher and coach whose passion for helping his student-athletes was matched only by his commitment to his craft. It's no surprise his teams were so successful. On weekends, our house filled up with his friends — teachers and coaches gathered around the TV to watch games and trade stories. As a sports-loving kid, I spent hours listening to them talk about their calling.

I've learned a lot about life through my journey in sports and am grateful for the time I've spent on the field with players, coaches, and teammates. Many of my closest friends are former teammates. I've played on about twenty-five teams and coached nearly thirty.

Not long ago, while working with a group of high school athletes, I asked them, "Why do you play sports?" The question seemed to catch them off guard. After a pause, a few tentative answers surfaced: "To get a scholarship," "To get recruited," "To win."

While playing sports can serve as a means to an end — earning a scholarship, getting recruited, or chasing wins — their real value runs much deeper. Sports are an end in themselves: a training ground for the qualities that shape character and make life meaningful. Young people learn to challenge themselves, trust others, and respond to failure. That's what sports were for me. I loved everything about them then and still do, though I sometimes worry we're losing sight of their true purpose.

I was never a professional athlete or coach, but I had my share of success. In high school, I played football, basketball, and lacrosse, earning top-athlete honors. In college, I was a three-time All-Conference selection, an All-American, and conference MVP while captaining a championship team. My athletic ability wasn't particularly remarkable — I was never the fastest kid on the playground — but my curiosity and willingness to keep learning set me apart.

My coaching career began almost by accident. After college, I was offered a two-year internship that combined writing athletic department press releases with being an assistant coach for the lacrosse team. It turned out to be the start of a lifelong calling.

I had the good fortune to assist my head coach, Ross Sachs — an uncommonly kind and thoughtful person — during his final season, then assisted G.W. Mix, a dynamic young coach who, in his head coaching debut, guided us to a conference title and the NCAA semifinals. Looking back, I couldn't have asked for better bookends to begin my journey: one embodying wisdom and calm, the other, competitive drive and creative energy.

At Governor's Academy, I carried their lessons

forward. Over twenty-one seasons, our teams won eight league titles. In my final eleven years, as my approach matured, we won 162 of 178 games. But the numbers only tell part of the story. The real reward was watching young athletes grow — learning, leading, and finding their own way through the game and through life. I grew a lot during that time, too.

I also had my share of failure. As the quarterback of my high school football team, I lost every game over two seasons. It was a humbling experience — physically exhausting, emotionally draining, and heavy to carry at sixteen or seventeen. I felt responsible for our struggles and embarrassed by our record. Yet that crucible tested my resilience and awakened something in me. I wanted to understand what it truly meant to lead, to persevere — to win. In time, those two winless seasons became a turning point. The disappointment I felt then fueled the discipline and drive I carried into college, where I was determined to fully realize my potential as an athlete.

Over the years, I've watched sports change — from the push toward early specialization and the focus on college recruiting to the booming world of NCAA and professional sports, and the steady, insidious advance of online betting.

Through it all, sports have been a constant in my life. I coached my own kids and shared their heartbreak when their mother passed away from cancer during their teenage years. Our teams and community enveloped us with love and compassion. Later, as a proud dad, I watched my children compete as college athletes.

In every chapter — through loss, change, and celebration — I've leaned on the lessons sports have given me.

My teammates have had my back since we first met on the field, and many of my closest friends and mentors came into my life through the game.

After my wife's passing in 2014, I turned to mindfulness and meditation to manage my grief. The practices proved so transformative that I earned my teaching certification and began sharing them with athletes and coaches. That experience opened my eyes to the mental challenges athletes face today — including performance anxiety, social media pressure, and burnout — while deepening my own understanding of sport and life.

In that context, what I find so powerful about sports is that they can be a pathway — one that leads us to a deeper understanding of the mind, and through that understanding, to heal, grow, and know ourselves more fully. And because sports belong mostly to the young, they help shape habits that last a lifetime: resilience, curiosity, optimism — qualities we need in a world that's constantly changing and often chaotic.

If you're an athlete, this book offers practices that can help you perform better and enjoy the game more. If you're a coach, it may help you see your role as mentor and leader in a new light. If you're a parent, it can help you support your young athlete with more understanding and compassion. And if you're simply someone who loves sport, I hope it reconnects you to the instinct for play, movement, and collaboration. There's an athlete in all of us. Sometimes we just need to find it.

This book is not a memoir, but a reflection and an offering — a reflection on a lifetime in sport as a player, coach, parent, and teacher, and an offering to see sport as a platform for lifelong growth, presence, and leadership.

Looking back now, I can see how every practice, every victory, and every loss was part of something larger — something that still moves through me today. The games, the people, the quiet moments before the first whistle, and the gatherings that followed — they live within me still, changing shape but never losing their hold. Over time, reflection has shown what I couldn't see back then: that meaning reveals itself slowly, deepened by perspective and distilled in memory.

I couldn't have written this as a younger man.

PART ONE

THE WHY: FINDING YOUR MOTIVATION, VALUES, AND MINDSET FOR THE JOURNEY

WHAT'S YOUR WHY?

DISCOVERING THE PURPOSE BEHIND PLAY

Have you ever wondered why you started playing sports in the first place? When I asked a group of high school students this question, their answers included: "to get a scholarship," "to get recruited," and "to win a championship." Most of them didn't have an answer, and they all looked confused about why I was asking. It's an important question. Make it a habit to regularly question how you spend your time. After all, you gradually become what you pay attention to. If you're reading this and aren't sure why you play sports, maybe it's time to pause and reflect.

Securing a scholarship, getting recruited to a college, and winning are all positive outcomes for athletes. However, I would argue that they shouldn't be the main reasons you play sports, and if they are, you won't play your best.

If, on the other hand, you are motivated from within, if you see playing sports as a way to challenge yourself, learn about who you are, and discover what you have inside, then you're on the right track. If you play sports because you enjoy the feeling of improvement, like the process of getting better at something, and yes, because you enjoy working hard and winning, then I believe not only will this journey benefit you, but you're also more likely to earn a scholarship, get recruited, or win the league championship.

Playing sports offers enough intrinsic benefits. View your involvement in sports as a journey of self-discovery and personal growth. If scholarships, fame, and money come your way, be grateful for those extra rewards.

∼

WHAT'S YOUR GIFT?
RECOGNIZING WHAT COMES NATURALLY TO YOU

No two people are identical. As an athlete, you should recognize that you have certain physical and mental qualities that are unique to you. Maybe you've always been one of the fastest kids on the playground, or one of the strongest. You might have excellent hand-eye coordination and be good at catching things. It could be your determination or your ability to fit seamlessly into a group and do what needs to be done.

You are a combination of qualities. If you can recognize your unique set of strengths, you can steer yourself toward situations that capitalize on those qualities. If you're skilled at shooting, then you need to focus on being available for the shot. You might have a talent for leadership. How can you best develop that skill and apply it? Or maybe you prefer to play a supporting role and stay out of the spotlight. Whatever it is, whoever you are, try to understand it and find ways within your sport to leverage it. In my case, I was quick but not fast. I had good anticipation skills and could catch and shoot. I found a role on my team where I could effectively use my strengths.

It's important to recognize both your strengths and weaknesses. Accept yourself as an athlete for who you are, and avoid comparing yourself to others. Focus mostly on developing your natural talents while working to improve your weaker areas.

The universe created only one of you for a reason. Just be you. That's your gift to humanity and to yourself.

~

PURPOSE
WHERE MEANING MEETS MOTIVATION

P urpose is a powerful motivating force. Think about it — how often do you hear a champion athlete or coach talk about a greater purpose during interviews? When LeBron James returned to Cleveland, he promised to bring a championship to a city that hadn't seen one since 1964. Two years later, he fulfilled that promise, dedicating that championship to Cleveland.

Having a greater purpose beyond your personal success can increase your motivation. It's worth asking: Why do we tend to try harder when our efforts serve a higher purpose? You are naturally wired as a social creature to be altruistic, not selfish.

At a basic level, you can focus your efforts on helping the team. Alternatively, you might choose another person, a group, an organization, a city, or a town. Maybe there is a cause that lends added meaning to your efforts, such as helping the disabled, oppressed, elderly, or sick.

Consider taping a picture of someone who motivates

you in your locker as a reminder before every practice and game that it's all bigger than you somehow.

There are plenty of good reasons to give your best every day. Connecting your effort to a person or cause makes it more meaningful. You might even inspire your teammates to work together toward these goals.

With purpose, you understand your connection to something much bigger than your "small" self. Purpose gives you more energy and motivation.

~

FAITH

TRUSTING THE PATH YOU CAN'T SEE

"*F*aith is taking the first step even when you don't see the whole staircase" —Dr. Martin Luther King Jr.

Part of playing sports is becoming comfortable with not knowing what the outcome will be. Each time you enter the arena, you can't be certain of the result, yet you continue to put yourself out there and try. In doing so, you develop faith — the idea that things will be OK, even if you're not quite sure how. Having faith in yourself and in your team is a first step toward success. Without faith, your confidence may falter, and at the first sign of trouble, you might fall apart. Faith helps you stay the course despite challenges. Faith makes you resilient.

Without a doubt, at some point, you will be behind in a game or race. Having faith gives you the energy to keep trying. It buys you time until something changes and you start to find success. And even in failure, faith is a wonderful virtue to cultivate. It's also contagious, like many emotions. Sometimes, having just one strong team member with faith is enough to inspire the rest of the team to follow suit.

Your character will be tested when things aren't going your way. Develop your faith. It will serve you well on and off the field.

ACCEPTANCE
MEETING REALITY AS IT IS

We tend to suffer when we wish what's happening right now was different — better somehow. Yet we can't ever change what's happening in *this* exact moment. Instead, we can work in this moment to change how some future moments might be. Carl Jung famously said, "What we resist, persists." By resisting something that feels unpleasant, we actually give it more power.

As an athlete, there will be times when what's happening in the moment feels difficult. You might be losing, for example. Or maybe you're in the middle of a tough practice session and your body is aching. Or you're injured. Wishing that wasn't the case won't change anything. Accepting that things are this way, while also working to improve future conditions, is the wise course of action here. Wishing you weren't performing poorly only makes the hurt worse and increases the likelihood of continued poor performance.

Wishing your current reality were different from what it is is like being at war with yourself. So, give up the war and try a different approach. Accept your current situation for what it is, and focus on the present moment to make future outcomes as positive as possible.

Fighting reality is a loser's game. Accepting reality while working to improve future outcomes is a winning mentality.

GRATITUDE
GROUNDING SUCCESS IN APPRECIATION

" *A noble person is mindful and thankful of the favors he receives from others"* —The Buddha

It's easy to overlook the many things we can be grateful for, focusing instead on what's wrong rather than what's right and good in life. Deliberately feeling grateful helps you shift from dwelling on what's wrong with your world to recognizing and appreciating all the good that's already present. The feeling of gratitude is one of openness and expansion, rather than contraction.

Athletes who regularly practice gratitude tend to feel less stress and anxiety because they start from a place of *enough*. When you cultivate gratitude, it becomes easier to notice when you've been helped. A team of grateful individuals functions well and smoothly. While there are always areas for growth and improvement, it's important to view those relative shortcomings within the context of the whole. Be grateful for your friends, family, coaches, school, team, health, and your abilities.

Be grateful for the opportunity to experience this world each day when you wake up.

It's nearly impossible to feel down when you practice gratitude. Make practicing gratitude a regular part of your day. Additionally, try to cultivate that feeling so it becomes a more consistent part of your character.

~

HUMILITY
STAYING GROUNDED IN SUCCESS AND STRUGGLE

Being humble means recognizing your strengths and weaknesses, being honest about yourself, and truly remaining modest. A humble athlete reaches greatness but doesn't see himself as great. He understands that greatness comes from humility, which says, "I can always improve."

Being humble involves regularly checking your ego for signs that it's becoming too big. The humble athlete feels excited about success but doesn't celebrate herself openly. Instead, she acknowledges others who have helped her along the way. Humility promotes a realistic, down-to-earth attitude, showing that she's coachable and approachable. At the highest levels, these athletes remember their roots and take time to help others. These humble leaders become team captains.

A humble athlete acknowledges their gifts when successful, and when not, patiently perseveres in their work, day after day. A team full of humble athletes respects opponents, accepts both success and failure with grace, recognizes that there's something bigger than the sport, and maintains perspective in all situations.

Humility is at the heart of improvement, growth, and leadership. Always be humble.

PATIENCE
LETTING THE GAME COME TO YOU

Having practiced mindfulness and meditation for over a decade, one of the most valuable qualities I have developed is patience. As an athlete, it's natural to feel impatient; you want to improve faster. As a coach, you want your team to perform at its best *now*. Yet by simply *wanting* things to be better — without investing the time and effort — we undervalue the *process*. You must understand that focusing on doing the work in the present moment will lead to success. Be comfortable with dedicating time to the process, knowing that you'll either achieve the desired results or make significant progress by remaining committed.

Often in sports, a specific action triggers an instant reaction. Sometimes the immediate response is perfect; other times, it's driven by emotion and impulsivity. A classic example is a team becoming impatient about scoring and letting that impatience lead to "forcing" play, ultimately failing to score. As a mindful athlete, you can learn to relax, providing time and space between stimulus and response. In this space, you can allow your body and mind to take the *right action* as the circumstances require. Sometimes, the right action is *non-action* — simply letting things be as they are, and not forcing them. Sometimes, you have to let the game come to you. You have to be fast, but not in a hurry.

So too must you be patient with yourself. Don't expect immediate improvement. Instead, stick to your plan of practice, knowing that if you stay faithful and patient with the process, the results you want will come in time. Sometimes, too, the solution to the challenge is revealed in moments of peace, when your intuition and body's natural intelligence can come forth. Patience allows for this.

"Between stimulus and response, there is a space. In that space is our power to choose our response. In our response lies our growth and our freedom." - Viktor Frankl

∾

Never Give Up
Resilience as a Daily Decision

In March of 2014, my wife was very ill and nearing the end of her 13-month battle with cancer. During a team cookout, I asked her if she wanted to say anything to the team. In her quiet voice, she told them to "Never Give Up." Our team was very much like a family, and she was close to the players and their parents.

She passed away a few weeks later, and in our final game of the season, we found ourselves down 9-6 with eight minutes left against the top team in the league. I called a timeout. During that short break, the team gathered in a tight huddle. It was quiet — I couldn't find the words to properly express myself. I talked about finishing strong. We looked each other in the eye. We silently acknowledged a feeling of confidence and urgency. Just before we broke the huddle, one player said, "There's no way we're losing this game! No f'ing way." We broke the huddle, shouting "Never Give Up."

We scored a minute later. Their focus was palpable. Holding off a determined opponent, we scored again a few minutes later, then tied the game with about a minute remaining. We won in overtime.

It's hard to describe in words the energy shift that occurred during the timeout. The team transformed the poignancy they were feeling in those moments into perfect execution. They played with great purpose. They never gave up.

It's a vital lesson. You know what the outcome will be if you give up. But if you keep fighting, keep trying, keep believing in each other, and stay present in the moment, there's no telling what could happen. It's always worth putting in your best effort until the final whistle blows. That's how we should live our lives.

"Never give up, for that is just the place and time that the tide will turn." - Harriet Beecher Stowe

CONFIDENCE
BUILDING SELF-TRUST THROUGH PREPARATION — AND PAYING IT FORWARD

C onfidence and faith are like cousins; they are closely related but distinct. Confidence comes from knowing that you are prepared and ready to face the challenge at hand. It's a strong, settled feeling that, no matter what, you'll be OK because you can handle it. You can manage the pressure, intensity, and physical demands of your sport. This confidence comes from training hard and training well. Confidence is a by-product of practice.

As a coach, I found that my athletes felt confident not because of emotional pep talks before the game or at half-time, but rather from being well-prepared, knowing they had the ability to execute and adapt to evolving circumstances.

The day before my first college game, my coach, Ross Sachs, told me I'd be starting. By that point in his career, he was older and quite experienced. He looked like a wise old coach. He didn't announce this in his office or post it somewhere; instead, he just walked up to me, smiled, put his arm around me, and said I'd be starting. Then he grinned broadly and looked me in the eye. In this way, he gave me real confidence. At that time, I was still a little unsure of myself as an athlete. I played well in that first game, and the older players patted me on the back and congratulated me. I never looked back, all thanks to Coach Sachs and the confidence he gave me.

We all can inspire confidence in others. Whether you're a teammate, parent, business owner, or community leader, demonstrating confidence in someone else is an act of kindness and leadership. It brings out the best in others.

Confidence is built on preparation. Whether alone or with a team, give your best and most consistent effort to preparation, and your confidence will grow. Demonstrating confidence in others encourages their development and is a vital part of leadership.

COURAGE
ACTING IN THE PRESENCE OF FEAR

When you step onto the athletic arena, you can't really be sure of the outcome. This in itself requires courage. Putting yourself out there in front of your parents, friends, and fans without knowing if you'll succeed can be daunting – and exhilarating. Repeating this process builds courage within you. Indeed, persevering in the face of challenges and defeat *is* courage.

Your athletic journey will give you many chances to be courageous. At some point, you'll face a heavily favored opponent. Can you find the courage to give your best effort? You might be physically overmatched. Can you stand up to that? Can you compete despite that reality? One of the great things about sports is that it offers many opportunities to be courageous. Life will also test your courage. Use your athletic journey to grow as a courageous person. You have nothing to fear.

. . .

Life is full of underdog success stories. Learn to thrive even when the odds are against you. Practice being courageous, and you'll become a courageous person.

~

IDENTITY
MORE THAN THE JERSEY YOU WEAR

You probably derive some or most of your identity from your sport. For example, you might say, "I'm a soccer player." It's easy to get caught up in that. When your identity as a person becomes too closely linked to your sport, you're shortchanging your self-worth. You are a multi-dimensional human being who *also* plays sports. And let's be real here – your competitive athletic career may likely end before you're 22 years old.

If you've staked too much of your self-worth in your identity as an athlete, where will you be when that part of you disappears? Will you feel empty and depressed that your athletic career ended too soon? Or will you realize that you are so much more than just a competitive athlete, allowing that part of you to fade away while you carry all the lessons from that journey into the rest of your life?

Athletics isn't who you are, but it's a powerful tool for building the best parts of yourself - the determination, the skill, the drive, the selflessness, and more. Remember, you can always be an athlete. Just don't let it consume too much of your identity.

You're a multi-dimensional human being who also happens to be an athlete. Develop all aspects of yourself, including your athleti-cism. Let all parts of yourself shine through and allow for new parts to emerge.

～

VALIDATION
PROVING YOU MATTER THROUGH EFFORT
AND GROWTH

F or many athletes, playing sports provides *validation*.
As I mentioned in the introduction, after failing as a
high school quarterback, I sought — and found — validation in college as a lacrosse player. For me, validation was
an incredibly motivating force. I had to prove myself *to
myself*.

My mentor, Johnny O'Brien, summed it up for me
when I talked about this book with him. Johnny was
orphaned at age three, when he and his brother were
dropped off at the Milton Hershey School after a family
tragedy. As he told me, sports became a way for him to
show, "I matter."

After a highly successful run as a student and athlete at
Milton Hershey, he became the starting tailback for an
undefeated Princeton team. Later, he worked with my
father as a teacher and coach, then went on to start a
successful management consulting firm, which he led for
many years. Finally, he became the head of the Milton

Hershey School, the very school where he began his unique and inspiring journey.

Sports provide many benefits to people, including the opportunity to prove oneself. In doing so, it can create a foundation for ongoing growth and leadership, as was the case for Johnny O'Brien.

POSITIVE SHIFT
CHOOSING OPTIMISM AS A TRAINED RESPONSE TO ADVERSITY

Your mind's main goal is to keep you safe, and it will go to great lengths to do this. No doubt you've felt the tendency to tell yourself that it's OK to cut your workout short or skip it altogether. Or maybe you've experienced your mind planting seeds of doubt, like "you probably won't win, so don't bother trying too hard," or "why bother trying out for the varsity, you probably won't make it anyway."

Your mind talks to you constantly. For most people, about two-thirds of that talk is negative. A key factor in being a successful athlete — and a successful person — is developing the habit of expecting success; of anticipating something positive to happen. For most people, making a habit of positive thinking takes effort and practice.

If you become self-aware enough to recognize your thought patterns, you can learn to change them. You are the captain of your ship, metaphorically speaking, and if your ship has drifted off course due to negative thought patterns, you can steer it back. Start by identifying a negative thought for what it is — simply a negative thought. Be kind to yourself and understand that this negative thought is often part of a hard-wired system designed to protect you.

Once you're aware, you can learn to let go of or reduce the time spent on that negative thought, leaving more space for positive ones. You might even try following that negative thought with a positive one. For example, instead of thinking a rainy day is bad, think about how much we need the water. And we need rainy days to truly appreciate the sunny ones. You can learn to develop this mindset, gradually becoming a more optimistic person. But you have to practice.

Optimism creates the conditions for all good things to happen. In this way, it's closely linked to faith — having a feeling that good things will occur without knowing exactly how. So practice cultivating those optimistic thoughts, words, and actions. It builds on its own momentum.

"Optimism is true moral courage." —*Sir Ernest Shackleton*

～

PART TWO

THE INNER GAME: MASTERING ATTENTION, THOUGHTS, EMOTIONS, AND PRESENCE

Your Mind and Performance

Where Champions Are Truly Made

How important is your mind to your performance? I ask this question every time I start working with an individual athlete or team. Without exception, they'll say it is very important. For illustrative purposes, I ask them to tell me what percent of their performance is based on their mental state. I now have a fairly large sample size, and the average comes in at around 80%. My next question is this: "So if 80% of your performance has to do with your mind, what percentage of your practice time do you spend training it?" This is when the players and coaches look down awkwardly, glance around the room, shake their heads, and mutter "none." Herein lies the opportunity.

Embrace the journey of training your mind. The benefits are endless and extend far beyond the playing field.

〜

YOU ARE NOT YOUR THOUGHTS
LETTING GO OF INNER NOISE

Here's a simple yet profound idea: *You* are not *your thoughts*. How often do you become anxious, regretful, or sad because of your thoughts? How does it make you feel to believe the negative self-talk that runs through your mind, particularly after making a mistake? The good news is that you are not your thoughts. You actually have a choice in the matter.

You can learn to treat thoughts as you do other sensory experiences. Just like a sound that arises, is noticed, and then disappears, thoughts can do the same. For example, you might notice a car approaching as you sit outside. It starts faint, gets louder, then fades away entirely. Thoughts behave similarly — if you allow them. However, too often when a thought, especially a negative one, appears, you tend to cling to it, hold onto it, and keep it around. These thoughts seem "sticky."

You can practice noticing when a thought arises, and as soon as you do, prevent yourself from attaching to it, letting it fade away just like the sound of the car. Maybe you can't stop it from arising, but you can learn to let it pass quickly.

Think about the implications here for you as an athlete. You may notice yourself getting fixated on the score in a close game. This triggers anxiety and fear of losing, which in turn affects how you play because you get tight and tentative. However, now you've been practicing having a "slick mind," releasing negative thoughts immediately after they appear. This allows you to stay in the moment as the game unfolds. Your focus is better, which means you play better.

Put thoughts in the same realm as vision, hearing, taste, felt sense, and smell. After all, thoughts show up in the same place. Learn to objectify them as diversions that come and go. Don't let them have power over you.

~

PRESENCE
THE POWER OF BEING FULLY HERE

Presence is the opposite of distraction and results from deep focus. It is a fully embodied state of being where you are unified with your current moment-to-moment experience. Almost every student or athlete will say they've had a teacher or coach who tells them to focus. However, in my experience, few, if any, can say that a teacher or coach has ever taught them *how* to focus. This can be frustrating — not knowing how to do the very thing you know you need to do.

I recall being a young pitcher during my Little League days. Anyone who's ever pitched knows how lonely it can be out there on the mound. You're right there in the middle of it all, trying to throw that ball past batter after batter. Much of the team's success rests on your ability to do that.

My dad would go to most of my games. Sometimes, between pitches, especially if I were becoming erratic, I'd hear him yell to me: "Concentrate!" And while he was well-intentioned, I really had no idea how to do that, which often just made the problem worse.

Many athletes learn to focus through trial and error. You might stumble upon the realization that you played really well and seemed to be totally present with it all. You might even realize that you have some control over it, which you do. In fact, your presence is always available to you. Your presence is your fundamental consciousness. It is your state of being before distracting thoughts appear.

The trick to being present is as much a passive act as an active one. In a sense, you're simply letting go of whatever distractions are stealing your focus. Shifting your attention from your thoughts to your breath — from your mind to your body — is a good way to do this. And when you can learn to let go of distraction, then you're really on to something. This is a skill that can be learned and practiced at any time.

When you catch yourself in a state of distraction, gently return to focusing on what's really happening right now, in this current moment of life.

~

DISTRACTION
SEEING WHAT DRAWS YOU AWAY
FROM NOW

Distraction is an enemy of performance. We all fall somewhere on the distractibility spectrum. Some people are extremely distracted, their minds aimlessly jumping from one thing to another. From my experience, both personally and as a meditation teacher, this is true for most of us. Then there are the fortunate few who seem capable of naturally staying focused on the task at hand, whether that's work, conversation, or play.

Distraction pulls our attention away from what is really happening in a particular moment. It is impatient, rude, sneaky, and highly effective at stopping us from fully engaging in the current moment — whether at work, rest, practice, or socializing. For distraction, *this moment* is never enough and always needs to be improved or changed.

For athletes, distraction takes many forms and pulls attention away from the game. It might appear as anxious thoughts or pregame jitters, like "Will I do OK today?" or in-game worries about mistakes, pleasing or disappointing others, fans watching, or random thoughts unrelated to the game. Distraction can greatly impact performance. It also blocks deep learning off the field, being an engaged social partner, or simply thinking clearly.

You live in a world that constantly tries to distract you. Recognize this and bring focus and intention to your life. You are responsible for your attention. Use it to your advantage.

MEDITATION
ACTIVELY TRAINING THE MIND TO BE STILL

M editation is essentially the practice of focus. It helps you develop the ability to observe your thoughts objectively, rather than identifying with them. For example, rather than clinging to negative self-talk after a mistake, like: "I can't believe you missed that shot. You suck," you learn to see that thought as just an appearance, which soon fades away, creating space for you to fully connect with the present moment. Meditation is a purposeful practice of watching what appears in consciousness.

When we meditate, we might focus closely on our breath. What does it feel like just to sit and breathe? We notice sensations arising in our bodies. Similarly, we can observe thoughts emerging and categorize them alongside physical sensations. This realization helps us understand that our thoughts are not who we truly are; they are merely appearances in consciousness — the same space where sights, sounds, smells, tastes, and physical sensations appear. Since most people tend to have more negative thoughts than positive ones, it's useful to see these thoughts as temporary and, by their very nature, destined to dissipate. We don't have to believe or identify with the stories they tell.

Athletes who practice meditation gradually train themselves to stay present, avoid getting lost in their thoughts and the stories they tell, and let their bodies perform as trained.

The ability to create some separation between yourself and your thoughts is an incredibly valuable life skill.

Meditation is the intentional practice of being present. It's worth sitting quietly and simply noticing what happens. Each meditation session helps you become more present in your natural state of being.

~

SELF-TALK
SHAPING PERFORMANCE THROUGH INNER DIALOGUE

Have you ever noticed that you go about your day having a conversation with an invisible "you" who seems to follow you around, judging and commenting — often negatively — on what you're doing? Have you ever noticed how this voice becomes louder and more critical when you make a mistake? This voice can be crippling, paralyzing you with fear. What if I mess up and let the team down? What if I don't play well in front of the college scouts? One of the most common questions I'm asked is: How do I deal with negative self-talk?

Well, you probably won't be able to eliminate self-talk entirely. The good news is that you can learn to shift the narrative from critical and negative to neutral, or even better, positive and encouraging. To do this, you need to become aware of your self-talk as it happens. You can expect that it will arrive loud and clear after you make a mistake.

It's worth noting that our brains naturally tend to focus on negativity and worry. Psychologists call this the "negativity bias" and believe it is a survival mechanism deeply embedded in our DNA. Essentially, the caveman who feared that the noise in the woods was a lion, hid in his cave and survived, while the caveman who thought it was a good idea to check out the noise, was likely eaten by the lion, preventing him from passing on his genes.

The good news about your brain exists in a fancy word called *neuroplasticity* — the fact that your brain is constantly evolving in response to experience. You can use this to your advantage by actively changing the tone in your self-talk from negative to positive. This will take some effort, but it will be worth it and will stick with you long after you stop playing sports.

It is helpful to think about what words would be most encouraging to hear after making a mistake. What could help you move forward? I ask athletes to write down a few words or a short phrase that they memorize and repeat to themselves, like: "It's OK, you're good, you got this." Start saying this to yourself. Build this habit by speaking positively to yourself. When you make a mistake, learn from it and move forward; don't keep replaying it and beating yourself up.

Learn to treat yourself as you would your best friend. See the silver lining behind the dark cloud. Have compassion for yourself. Create a positive mantra that you say to yourself in the wake of a mistake. Post it in a visible place. Say it to yourself a lot.

FEAR

FACING WHAT SCARES YOU — AND FINDING LIGHT IN IT

F ear will definitely be part of your athletic journey. You might worry about failing, disappointing your teammates or parents, getting hurt, or putting it all out there on the line and not succeeding.

Fear is a strong emotion that can control your life if you don't confront it. You need to learn not only to face your fears but also to transform them. The opposite of fear is love, so developing this feeling can help dispel fear from your heart. Shift your perspective to love — love for the game, your team, the competition, and the whole journey you're on together. Find a way to accept the entire experience as if it were a precious gemstone because, in a way, it really is. And you're lucky to have it.

Take a moment to appreciate how fortunate you are to have a healthy, strong body and the opportunity to compete. Focus on your relationships with teammates, coaches, family, or friends. Really invest in those special bonds you've built. Replace any feelings of fear or scarcity with a sense of love and abundance. This will help you feel better and perform at your best.

Don't let fear run your life. If you can identify your fears and face them, you'll find that they fade away. Fear lives in darkness. Shine the light of love on it.

~

PRESSURE
LEARNING TO BEND WITHOUT BREAKING

Playing sports naturally creates pressure. As young athletes grow, the pressure to win and perform well intensifies. Unfortunately, even very young athletes experience unnecessary stress as parents and fans turn ordinary youth league games into intense drama.

Some might argue that pressure can be helpful because it promotes change. Like a pressure cooker in the kitchen, added pressure can speed things up. But is that always a positive? It's important to see that pressure can also cause damage. When too much weight is put on a weak foundation, the structure collapses.

For athletes, the emotional foundation should be built gradually. It's OK for young players to struggle under pressure as long as they receive full support from caring parents and coaches. After all, life also presents pressure, and even the strongest among us can break sometimes. The main lesson here is that sports can teach us how to manage pressure and turn it into a positive force to build resilience.

Finally, pressure is, to some degree, self-induced. We often generate pressure by overemphasizing the importance of winning and flawless performance. Ironically, the athletes who perform the best are those who have learned to release that pressure. They learn to handle pressure by accepting the way things are and getting excited to perform their best. Worrying too much only adds to the pressure.

Learn to view pressure as a force that strengthens your resilience. Recognize that most pressure is self-induced, and learn to release it when necessary.

～

Rest
The Overlooked Discipline of Recovery

E verything in nature needs rest. There can be no activity without rest. Rest comes before activity; activity follows rest. It's simple. Unfortunately, too many athletes are shortening their rest periods in favor of more activity. This is counterintuitive and leads to diminishing returns, or even worse. More isn't always better. It's the quality that counts.

The body needs rest to stay healthy. For young athletes who expend a lot of energy, getting enough sleep is essential for recovery. It's fine to train hard, but those workouts must be balanced with adequate sleep and rest.

When athletes don't get enough rest, they build up a physical and mental deficit. Being under-rested makes athletes more prone to injury, increases irritability, and reduces focus. You probably know what it's like to push through a tough practice on too little sleep. You also know what it feels like to wake up feeling completely rested.

It's important to be aware enough to recognize when

your body needs rest. Ideally, you follow a routine that allows for a consistent amount of sleep each night, avoiding late nights and early mornings.

You are an athlete through your body. Make sure it gets enough rest.

PROCRASTINATION
LEARNING TO MEET AVOIDANCE DIRECTLY

Sport is an act of doing. You can't imagine your way through a game; you actually have to play it. Sport is a physical act in the same way that mowing the lawn or writing a term paper is a physical act. Procrastination is the enemy of action. It is the opposite force, and a strong one at that.

So often, we know we should do something, yet we keep putting it off, only to realize that it wasn't so bad, maybe even enjoyable, when we finally did it. When we allow ourselves to negotiate with that part of our mind that tells us to wait, the result is inaction. Often, this inaction can evoke feelings of guilt and even shame for not doing what you need to do.

Train yourself to do the things you need to do. Start small, like getting up when your alarm goes off and making your bed. Look for small victories each day in your fight against the force of procrastination. Break down the big, scary project into small, manageable chunks and chip away at progress. Create to-do lists and generate some forward momentum. Get up off the couch and do something.

The more you practice pushing through procrastination, the better you'll get at it.

A body in motion tends to stay in motion. A body at rest tends to stay at rest. Keep moving. Go out and live your life.

THINKING VS. DOING
BRIDGING INSIGHT WITH ACTION

Our active minds love to think, constantly predicting the future and getting lost in the past. With mindfulness, we aim to keep our attention on our experience as it happens, rather than before it occurs or after it's over. For athletes, it's easy to get caught up in the excitement of the upcoming game or practice session.

Many athletes spend a lot of time thinking about how to improve, whether through skills training, conditioning, or gaining a better understanding of their sport. The mind enjoys this *thinking about doing*. In a way, we can even feel a sense of achievement by thinking about doing something enough. However, we realize that no matter how much we review film, think, read scouting reports, etc., it all means nothing without action.

So, while it's good and even necessary to think about ways to improve, to "watch the film in our minds," so to speak, the game, like life itself, is an action sport. There-fore, it's essential to be self-aware enough to know when it's time to shift from thinking to doing.

Similarly, I've seen many coaches talk too much to their players, wasting valuable practice time. Clearly, coaches must explain how players can improve, what they need to do, and how to run drills, among other things. They also need to remember that sports are movement-based physical activities, and therefore, players must repeatedly practice the movements related to their sport.

In life, we learn by doing, and sports are no different.

Thinking can be productive if followed by action. Thinking about doing something and then not doing it can make you feel inadequate. You can't do everything, so focus on your priorities and follow through.

~

SELF-DISCIPLINE
DOING THE WORK WHEN NO ONE'S WATCHING

It's natural to see discipline as something difficult or negative. At its worst, discipline can be imposed on someone unfairly or even cruelly. But in its best form, discipline helps build good habits, correcting for negative patterns and behaviors. In sports, the coach is often the disciplinarian. Sadly, some coaches push this too far, using their authority in ways that can harm athletes.

The self-disciplined athlete understands the habits they want to develop, such as maintaining good nutrition, sticking to training routines and schedules, being punctual, and staying focused and positive. When you find yourself drifting away from these positive habits, you need to get back to the right behaviors. This is what being self-disciplined is all about.

You don't need a coach, parent, or teacher to tell you what to do; you know what to do. Set a high standard and hold yourself accountable. Self-discipline doesn't have to be hard or unpleasant. In fact, being self-disciplined is an act of self-care, and having a routine keeps you on track mentally and physically.

Self-discipline is key to your success as a person. It is essentially an act of self-care. You will face temptations to stray in many ways. Stay the course.

∼

THE QUIET WORK
WHERE TRUE MASTERY IS BUILT

The most successful athletes understand that they need to train much more than what an in-season practice schedule allows. So, they commit to doing the "quiet work." Quiet because it's not loud, not in the spotlight; in fact, often no one else even knows they're doing it. Still, the athlete shows up in the quiet place to do the quiet work, motivated by the intrinsic feeling of self-improvement.

Can you, as an athlete, no longer caught up in end results, lose yourself in the calm, steady process of improvement? Can you find joy in feeling yourself improve through methodical, solitary practice?

When you love the feeling of progress, you want to keep at it. Improvement happens through tiny gains repeated again and again against the slow roll of time. You might ask yourself: what feels better afterward? An hour of scrolling social media on your phone, or an hour practicing your jump shot or serve? The quiet work of self-improvement is a lifelong journey that produces great results. Like a good investment, it compounds over time.

View the quiet work as sacred and spiritual. It's where you go to keep discovering yourself. That path is for you alone. No one can walk it for you.

~

SELF-EXPRESSION
WHEN SPORT BECOMES SONG

When we think of self-expression, we often picture an artist — a painter at work with watercolors, or a musician strumming a guitar and singing from the heart. We might imagine the grace of a dancer or the precision of a ballerina, each movement telling a story.

Playing sports can simply be another form of art. Many athletes feel most at home on the field, more themselves there than anywhere else. This was certainly my experience. The game becomes a space where emotion, instinct, training, and creativity meet. Through movement, rhythm, and flow, athletes express parts of themselves that words can't quite reach. In this way, sport becomes an act of creation and self-expression.

As a coach, I often told my players to see the field as their canvas and to paint something beautiful together. There's a real artistry in sport when it's played freely — when athletes lose themselves in the moment and the game seems to play through them. The speed, the energy, and the unpredictability all add to the creative experience.

Sport mirrors life. When we relax and fall into the flow, our true nature has room to emerge. Life, like sport, invites us to play — to create, to express — on a vast and ever-changing canvas.

View your sport as your art form — a way to express who you are. Let your individuality flow through the game, and see your training as the craft that shapes your expression.

LIKE WATER
ADAPTING SMOOTHLY TO EVERY CHALLENGE

When water flows down the mountainside during the spring melt, it doesn't know where it's headed. There's no set route, no specific plan. There's no chaos either, because there is no mind. Water simply follows the path of least resistance. When it encounters a rock in its way, it goes around. It keeps flowing, never truly stopping, even if still.

It flows into a stream, continues onward, reaches a river, and keeps moving until it finds the sea. Then, in the heat, it rises, only to fall as snow on another mountain many miles away.

As an athlete, embracing the mindset of water means trusting your intuition. It involves naturally moving toward open space, instinctively reaching into the passing lane, or sensing where your opponent is. Let your natural intelligence serve you. Don't let your mind block your instincts. Just flow, like water.

. . .

Sometimes the easiest path is the right one. When you move like water, you naturally go where you need to be.

THE FLIP
FINDING OPPORTUNITY IN A PERSPECTIVE SHIFT

This happens often. A team or individual athlete gets ahead in a game or race. As the game progresses and the finish line approaches, the team in the lead starts to think they will win, unconsciously relaxing. Sensing this, the trailing team doubles down and begins to catch up. This unsettles the leading team, causing them to doubt themselves, while the trailing team gains confidence. Eventually, it flips — the loser becomes the winner.

There are many lessons to learn from this common event. Most importantly, the game is never truly over until it's over. Every lead is temporary; its preservation depends only on continuing what has happened so far. However, each new moment in the game offers a fresh opportunity — for better or worse. Each moment is always "to be determined." A score during a game is just a temporary snapshot of where things stand at that time. It doesn't have to predict what happens next.

Teams and individual athletes known for holding leads and finishing strong excel at starting fresh with each moment, continuing to focus and do what helped them build their lead. They push right through the finish line and stay emotionally steady. This is difficult because the mind craves resolution — either a win or a loss — even while the game is ongoing. We want to know with some certainty what will happen, but being comfortable with uncertainty is what supports consistent good performance.

If you have the lead, play as if you're behind. If you don't have the lead, find the courage to believe you will win despite the current circumstances. Regardless of which side you are on, never give up.

Your mind is a "prediction machine" that uses past experiences to forecast future results. Challenging its often flawed reasoning creates room for new opportunities. Don't worry about your opponent — focus on yourself and stay dedicated to working hard in every game.

∽

RESET

BEGINNING AGAIN IN EACH NEW MOMENT

An aim of mindfulness practice is to become more present. When you're present, your attention is fully on what's happening in the moment. When you're not present, you're thinking about the future or reliving the past. As I neared the end of my coaching career and began to understand the power of mindfulness, I found myself in a coaching situation that required me to draw on this practice.

We had a young goalie who, despite performing well in early-season practice, struggled in our first game. I could tell he was nervous before his first start, and clearly, he let his mind get the better of him. I noticed that after he let in a goal, he would become mentally disengaged for a while.

Before the next game, I drew a red dot on his wrist with a Sharpie. I told him that this was his reset button, and after he let in a goal or realized negative self-talk was happening, he should push the button and take a few deep breaths while refocusing on whatever was happening. To help him refocus, he would try to focus intently on what he was seeing. In that way, he was able to get "out of his head" and into his body.

This move worked well for him, and he started playing better. After a while, many players began using the reset button. The season went great, the goalie played really well, and we ended up winning the league title, the last one of my career.

A few years later, with the support of my close friend and teammate, Rippy Philipps, I created an actual reset bracelet with an embedded clicker. This enabled me to share the idea with more people. Since then, I have sent reset bracelets to thousands — mainly athletes, but also teachers, therapists, nurses, and anyone looking for a simple wearable tool to help them stay present.

The reset bracelet helps people follow through on their intentions. It is a training tool that helps them understand and control their minds.

Every new moment offers a chance to reset and start over.

PART THREE

THE CRAFT: PRACTICE, PROCESS AND MASTERY

PRACTICE
THE HEARTBEAT OF GROWTH

In a sense, you are *always* practicing something, whether it's improving your athletic skill or sitting on the couch scrolling social media. This is critical to recognize and remember: You get better at what you do a lot. Think of it this way – whatever you do and think is strengthening a path in your neural circuitry. When my wife was ill and in the months after her passing, I was often sad and worried. It struck me that I was becoming more adept at being "sad and worried," much like I had developed skills in sports. I was conditioning my mind to those emotions.

To improve at something, you need to practice it intentionally. You know this from being an athlete. As you reflect on the words in this book, think about how you can turn these ideas into actions. Whether it's developing focus, optimism, or specific sports-related skills, remember that whatever you choose to practice — and it is a choice — you will get better at it. A related way to see this is that whatever you choose to pay attention to, you move closer to becoming.

To increase your endurance, run longer distances. If you want to shoot better, work on your shot. Suppose you want to be kinder — practice being kind. If you want to worry less, practice worrying less. Learn to make practices out of the ways you want to develop yourself mentally, physically, and spiritually. It's really not complicated, but it takes discipline and dedication.

Whether you realize it or not, you're always practicing something. Pick what you want to excel at — physically and mentally — and practice.

~

PERFECTING YOUR CRAFT

MASTERY THROUGH CONSISTENT, INTENTIONAL WORK

In sports, we constantly strive to perfect our craft. Perhaps you are trying to become more accurate in shooting a three-pointer, dribbling, hitting a spin serve in tennis, or making the perfect block in football. To become a good athlete in your sport, you need to hone your craft.

As humans, we have an innate desire to improve at what we do, an inherent drive to refine our skills. However, there is a subtlety I need to point out: There is a healthy way to pursue mastery and an unhealthy way. In an unhealthy way, we are always striving and grasping, judging ourselves against some vision of perfection — perhaps another athlete who appears perfect. It's essential to differentiate between comparing yourself to an unrealistic standard and genuinely enjoying the process of improvement, regardless of the outcome.

If you are blessed with natural physical gifts, you just may approach perfection someday. A few examples are Steph Curry's or Caitlin Clark's shooting ability, or Patrick Mahomes' uncanny knack for making the right play at the right time. However, for most athletes, the real value lies in the process of improvement. This becomes a lifelong gift — to stay curious about becoming a better friend, coworker, or parent — a quality that can be cultivated through sport.

You don't have to be perfect to be great. Greatness comes from striving for perfection while understanding that perfection might not be fully achievable.

~

GROWTH EDGES
LEARNING BEYOND THE BORDER OF COMFORT

Getting better at anything requires training at your "growth edge." What does that mean? Too often, I see athletes sticking to what they do best. For example, a baseball player might be excellent at hitting fastballs and then start waiting only for fastballs to swing at. That might work temporarily. But if that player understands that true growth comes from learning to hit curveballs, sliders, and changeups too, then they become a much tougher out.

It's easy to feel good in your athletic "comfort zone," but it's important to honestly assess your strengths and weaknesses and train at the edges. Make your training difficult. Use your off-hand more; take on the challenges that seem more difficult. This is how you grow both as an athlete and a person. Put yourself in tough situations, especially against better players.

When training alone, push yourself to the edge. If it feels too easy, make it harder. Growth always involves some discomfort (that's why it's called "growing pains").

The best athletes stay at their edge, continuing to grow and evolve.

Recognize when you're becoming too comfortable — physically and mentally — and make a habit of pushing yourself beyond that point. This is how you grow.

∾

NATURAL CURIOSITY
WHERE WONDER FUELS IMPROVEMENT

We are naturally curious from birth. Learning is hardwired into us. We have an inherent drive to explore, understand, and interact with the world in ways that help us make sense of it. This desire isn't just mental; our bodies instinctively want to move, play, dance, and physically explore the world around us.

Athletes need to stay curious. Mentally, they should continue to improve their understanding of their sport. What works? What doesn't? What small changes can I make to improve my play? Physically, athletes must continually enhance their bodies' performance within the sport. How does the body interact with the game? With teammates? With opponents?

When athletes integrate their mental and physical learning, they become whole in their athletic realm. This is a joy to watch.

. . .

Nurture your innate curiosity. Question your current assumptions by constantly asking if there are different ways to solve the problems you face. Allow your natural curiosity to guide you.

HANDS AND FEET
BUILDING SKILL FROM THE GROUND UP

Your hands and feet are crucial to your success as an athlete. After all, movement usually involves arms and legs. No matter which sport you play, developing your hands and feet is essential. Young athletes, in particular, should focus on building basic skills like footwork, catching, and throwing. Simply learning how to change direction smoothly can make a huge difference. Training your feet to cut properly, start, and stop is a foundational skill.

Unfortunately, many athletes lack the patience to dedicate enough time to footwork drills. It's simple and pays dividends in every sport. The same applies to hand skills. Learning to throw and catch correctly is critical and transfers across many sports. Improving dexterity, whether for rowing crew or hitting a golf ball, requires spending time developing hand skills.

Throwing and catching are effective ways to improve hand-eye coordination. It doesn't matter if you're tossing a tennis ball, a frisbee, a football, or even practicing juggling;

anything you do to develop your catching and throwing skills will pay off down the road in various ways.

Sports generally require dexterity and movement. Spend time developing your hands and feet.

TOOLS OF YOUR TRADE
HONORING THE GEAR THAT SHAPES
THE GAME

Just as an artist's brush becomes an extension of her hand, your equipment allows you to engage with your sport. In hockey, field hockey, and lacrosse, you use a stick; in rowing, an oar; and in baseball, a bat and glove. In soccer, your cleats are essential. There's a basketball, a football, or a sprinter's spikes. My point is that every sport has an instrument. How you interact with that instrument greatly shapes your success. Your skill with that instrument is honed over many hours of practice, and eventually, it becomes an extension of you.

As a young lacrosse player, I often dodged past imaginary defenders in my house — chairs, doorways, and the like. I practiced picking up anything off the floor with my stick, whether it was a ball, a toy, or even a paperclip. I kept the stick in my hand a lot. When I was growing up, it was common to see my friends dribbling a basketball down the street or walking along with a football in hand.

There's something about the time spent that's crucial here. You can't develop a true connection with your instrument without dedicating time to it. And you need to enjoy that time to truly appreciate it. You may find that time spent with your sports gear is more valuable than being online or watching a screen. You might discover that becoming really skilled at your sport involves under-standing the nuances of your equipment.

Be mindful of the instrument that links you to your sport. Spend time with it and learn to make it feel like an extension of your body.

~

MINDFULNESS OF THE BODY

LISTENING CLOSELY TO PHYSICAL WISDOM

I t's easy to believe that you *are* your mind. After all, our minds are so powerful, creating thoughts and stories we often assume to be true. We seem to live our lives through our minds. But do we, really? The Irish author James Joyce captures this idea when he says, "Mr. Duffy lived a short distance from his body." Joyce's short story "A Painful Case" describes a man living a life disconnected from his feelings — physical or otherwise.

Yet it all comes down to the body. After all, our brain, like our heart, is just part of our body. In mindfulness, we can shift our attention from the mind to the body.

"I was too in my head" is a phrase often used to describe subpar athletic performance. So, you need to get out of your head and into your body. When we shift our attention from our mind to the physical sensations in our body, something changes. We become more aware of the present moment and the physical experience of being alive.

As an athlete, you understand what it feels like to

become one with the process of playing the game. You reach a point where your focus is entirely centered, and your body responds during the game with nearly perfect precision. Your training takes over, and your body does what it needs to do without your mind interfering. You know what it's like to be in this flow state, where mind, body, and experience blend together seamlessly. With practice, you can learn to reach this state of flow every time you participate in your sport. You can also apply this practice to your life outside of the field.

As you train yourself to stay more in your body and less in your mind, you'll strengthen your connection to what is truly happening in the present moment. This is essential for athletic success because it requires clear focus.

Use your sports training to build a strong connection with your body, then carry this awareness into all parts of your life, even when you're not training or competing.

You are your body. If you pay attention to your body, your mind will follow. Affirm your body's natural intelligence. Calm your mind and allow your body to express itself.

～

INPUTS
GUARDING WHAT YOU TAKE IN — MIND, BODY, AND HEART

You should regularly assess your "inputs." You ask a lot of your body in terms of output, but what are you putting in? If you put in junk, you'll get junk out; if you put in quality, you'll get quality out. Over time, you become the sum of your inputs.

Consider all of your inputs. What are you eating? What are you looking at? What are you listening to? What are you feeling physically? You should eat high-quality, fresh food as much as possible, with plenty of fruits and vegetables. Your body needs healthy food, and enough of it. Whatever you look at leaves an impression. A walk in the woods or along a beach provides your mind with healthy visual stimuli. Listening to music can lift your spirits.

Wise or inspiring words in a good book also give the mind much-needed healthy input. If you consume too much social media, you'll likely find yourself comparing yourself to others. If you take in too much violent, hateful content, it will also pollute your mind. Be mindful of the physical spaces you inhabit. Decorate your living space with beauty and inspiration. Seek out the wise and read from their texts. Learn to appreciate the good and beautiful in all forms and incorporate them as much as possible into your environment.

Good output comes from good input. It just can't be expressed any other way. Surround yourself with quality inputs and protect yourself from bad ones.

~

INTENTION
ACTING WITH CLARITY AND PURPOSE

E ngaging with your sport as an athlete is a purposeful act. Therefore, it is important to be intentional about what you aim to achieve. The practices your coaches design are meant to help you reach a shared goal — performing your best both individually and as a team. When it's time to practice, set your intention to fully engage with the exercises, drills, and activities to maximize their benefit. This demands focus and discipline.

The same applies when you practice or work out alone or informally with a small group. Decide to make the most of this time. Engage completely with the work. Show your body that this is important work that must be done well. To set your intention, take a few minutes before practice to get excited about the opportunity and promise yourself to work hard, listen, observe, and learn.

Remember, every practice is a chance to improve. However, without setting an intention, your effort may falter, and you could just go through the motions, literally. That would be a waste of time.

· · ·

*Before starting something, set an intention to do it well and
wholeheartedly.*

~

PREPARATION
CONFIDENCE BORN FROM CONSISTENT WORK

When preparing for an opponent, you try to learn as much as possible about them, including their tendencies, patterns, and key players. You study film, scout an opponent in person, talk to others who have competed against them, etc. While these practices can be helpful, be careful not to let your focus shift from yourself to your opponent.

Earlier in my coaching career, I sometimes hyper-focused on an opponent before a big game. This caused several problems. We spent too much practice time on special strategies at the expense of sharpening our own skills. Over-focusing on the opponent distracted us from our own team's needs, ultimately hurting our preparation.

Preparing for an opponent also requires resources and staffing. At the college and pro levels, a team might have staff whose sole focus is to scout and plan against the opposition. A high school team, however, has limited time and staff. It's crucial to understand the best ways to utilize your resources here. Spending too much time discussing an upcoming opponent can make that opponent seem better than they really are. Don't worry about them too much.

If you can learn something about your opponent, you should. However, most of your time and focus should be on refining your strategies and leveraging your strengths.

"The art of war teaches us to rely not on the likelihood of the enemy not coming, but on our own readiness to receive him; not on the chance of his not attacking, but rather on the fact that we have made our position unassailable." - Sun Tzu

PLAYING TIME
EMBRACING YOUR ROLE AND CONTRIBUTION

I f you're like most athletes, playing time is on your mind. After all, playing in competition is what it's all about. Or is it? Over the years, I've worked with many athletes who are very focused on their playing time or whether they are in the starting lineup. The reality is that most rosters have three, four, or even five times as many players as the number in the starting lineup. It's also common for more players to not play than to actually get into the game. Of course, you want to be a starter, but I believe there's a better and healthier way to approach playing time.

How much you play is mostly beyond your control since it depends on your coaches' decisions. You might be a player who is just naturally talented enough that the coach finds it easy to play you. However, most players will likely face the eventual reality of not playing much, or not playing at all, at some point in their careers. If your goal is to be a starter but that decision is largely out of your hands, you're tying your happiness to something you can't control.

When this happens, you might start searching for someone or something to blame. Often, players blame the coach for not playing them. But coaches tend to be quite objective, trying to select the combination of players that gives the team the best chance to succeed. Some players might blame themselves for not getting enough playing time. This mindset is also unhealthy. Actually, it's no one's fault at all.

Your goal as a player should be to become the best you can be. Your satisfaction should come from the effort you put in and the progress you make in improving yourself. Don't make the mistake of tying your happiness to something you don't control.

Every level you advance — youth to high school, high school to college, college to pro — you join a more talented pool. At some point, you might find yourself surrounded by many players on your team who are a bit faster, stronger, or more skilled than you. And that's OK! You can only be the best you can be.

I've coached many athletes who excelled in high school but ended up with limited playing time in college. They practiced their hearts out, but with little to show for it in terms of playing time or stats. If you are one of these players, hear this: If you can stay positive, keep working hard, support your teammates from the bench, and give your all to the team knowing you might not play much or at all, then you'll be capable of anything in life because you will have learned what it truly means to be selfless. This is one of the most difficult yet most important lessons in sports.

. . .

Your worth as a player shouldn't be measured by stats or playing time, but by the effort you put into bettering yourself and the team, and the attitude you maintain. If you approach life this way, you'll always be a winner.

Process vs. Outcome

Freedom in Doing the Work, Not Chasing Results

Many factors contribute to peak athletic performance, including physical conditioning, coordination, strategic preparation, and effective execution. Athletes need to train and prepare to perform at their best. Yet there's something deeper and more fundamental here.

For athletes to perform optimally, they must be completely focused and fully present in each moment of their experience. This means that while competing, they ideally become one with the process. When this happens, an athlete's mind and body unify. Their training and conditioning support them, enabling them to react automatically — and perfectly — to the game's changing conditions. They aren't thinking about the outcome, nor dwelling on any mistakes they may have made. They allow their body and mind to work together in harmony.

How might this be incredibly useful beyond sports? What if you could approach your daily life the same way an athlete approaches competition? To be fully immersed in the process of living, allowing your innate wisdom to naturally come forth. To perform at your best in each moment as it happens, free of anxiety or self-doubt — *without fear.* To flow with the present, release your grip, and trust in your natural human perfection.

Just as an athlete trains for the game, we can train ourselves to become unified with the *process* of living. We can learn to stay focused on the present experience, responding in the most useful and synchronized way.

The process creates the outcome. Improve your methods and devote your full attention to them. Only then will you start to see your best results both on and off the field.

SIMPLICITY
SEEING THE WHOLE BEFORE THE PARTS

In spring 2003, one of my former players, JJ Morrissey, was a freshman at the University of Virginia, playing for legendary coach Dom Starsia. At that time, I was starting to find my footing as a coach after winning our first league title in 2002. I had become somewhat familiar with Dom through his recruitment of JJ and our interactions at summer camps and clinics, where I would occasionally chat with him.

I traveled to Charlottesville to watch Virginia play North Carolina. The day before the game, I asked Dom for a few minutes of his time for a whiteboard session. During that hour, he not only taught me some critically important tactics but, more importantly, he changed my perspective.

I quickly noticed that when I asked him a question, instead of answering in detail, he would first frame it in a big-picture, conceptual way. It dawned on me that as a coach, I could repeat the smaller details that I had learned, but to be a good teacher, I needed to ensure my players understood the concepts from which those details flowed.

Dom simplified things for me, communicating in a genuine and caring way. From then on, I always started coaching with the big picture in mind and gradually moved to the details. This approach helped my players truly understand how the game works at a basic level.

Based on what I learned about Dom's teaching methods, it was no surprise to me when they won the NCAA Championship that spring.

Too often in life, we overlook the essentials to focus on the details. In this information-overloaded society, it's easy to dive into the specifics without first understanding the larger concepts and reasons. As humans, we tend to over-complicate our lives. It's crucial to grasp the basics first, then proceed slowly from there.

In sports and life, begin with a broad understanding and then delve into details as needed.

∾

RESISTANCE
RECOGNIZING THE INTERNAL FRICTION
THAT TESTS COMMITMENT

Athletes know how it feels mentally before a tough workout or practice. The mind wants to protect the body, forming thoughts like "you don't need to do it today" or "gosh, this is gonna be so hard." It's easy to skip a workout or slack off during practice. When the mind yells, "Don't do it," that's resistance. Still, each workout and practice gives us a chance to recognize resistance and then push through it. Making this a habit trains us to consistently push through resistance toward our goals. During those moments, we "leave it all on the field." There's nothing to save for later.

Can you learn to recognize resistance for what it is? Your mind tells you to take it easy. Can you learn to objectify that thought instead of becoming identified with it? Practice recognizing, then pushing through the resistance. Only when this becomes a habit can you do great things.

. . .

Resistance is a force that tries to stop you from doing what you should do. The more you learn to push through it, the weaker it becomes. Don't negotiate with your mind.

COMMITMENT
THE QUIET, DAILY CHOICE TO KEEP SHOWING UP

Commitment means promising or agreeing to do something in the future, a firm and unwavering dedication to a pledge or course of action, even when facing difficulties. We often hear about commitment in the context of relationships. "I'm committed to doing this with you." It is a powerful word that represents an ideal. When we fully commit to something — whether it's a task or a relationship — we are telling ourselves that we are all in! As an athlete, it is critical to commit completely; if you approach a competition or even a practice with a weak sense of commitment, you won't perform well.

In some ways, a lack of commitment is like giving yourself an excuse to bail out. Making a full commitment can be intimidating. What if things don't really work out? However, it's through making these promises and sticking to them that you build character. So, whether you're part of a team or an individual athlete, think about what your commitment really means. Practice being committed every day. Go all in and see what happens. You might be pleasantly surprised by the outcome!

It's easy to hedge against full commitment. However, being partly committed never gets the job done. Go all in.

SEASONS
UNDERSTANDING THE NATURAL CYCLES OF GROWTH, AND RENEWAL

L ike the seasons of the year, athletic seasons have distinct segments. The preseason is the period before the competitive season begins and is loaded with anticipation, like Spring. Early season marks the start of the competitive journey, where players adjust to their roles and coaches decide what to focus on early.

Midseason, like summer, is when a team begins to really come to life — the adjustment period has passed, and the team is now learning and improving together, practice by practice, getting a little better each day. Losses happen, but they provide valuable opportunities for growth and learning.

Like fall, late season is when the team has matured, bonds are strong, and time is running out. It can be a meaningful time, as team members reflect on the colorful journey that is almost complete. It can also be a time of disappointment when early-season expectations clash with reality. Regardless, it is a time to savor the effort, the struggles, and the shared experiences that united the team.

Like winter, at season's end, things become still and quiet, allowing for rest and reflection before it all starts again.

An athletic season is a special experience that deserves respect and reverence. Life mirrors this in so many ways.

Take a holistic and patient approach. Keep the big picture in mind, but don't hesitate to break it down into manageable chunks. Remember, seasons change, and nothing is permanent —it's all part of life's natural cycle.

Luck

Accepting What's Out of Your Hands

Luck will always be a factor in your athletic life, just as it is in everyday life. No matter how much you try to control things, there will always be the odd bounce, a sudden gust of wind, or a rain shower in the middle of the game. Sometimes you can do everything right and still hit the post, miss the putt, or lose the race. Many variables in sports and life are outside of your control.

It's helpful to remind yourself of this. While you can control your effort, your dedication to training, and your attitude, there's much that's out of your hands. Sometimes luck is on your side, and sometimes it isn't. There's really nothing you can do to influence that. So focus on the parts that aren't affected by luck.

When luck is with you, be grateful; when it isn't, remember that things tend to balance out. Stay positive, and you'll more often than not find yourself on the right side of the luck equation.

. . .

Luck will always play a role in your life. We can never know what might happen next. Find comfort, not fear, in that fact.

PART FOUR

CONNECTION, COLLABORATION, AND LEADERSHIP: EXPANDING MASTERY BEYOND THE SELF

TEAMWORK
BECOMING BETTER TOGETHER

I often remind athletes how lucky they are to be part of a team. What a gift! Developing good teamwork skills will undoubtedly make you a better person. Humans are social creatures, and we must learn and practice how to be the best social beings we can be.

When you're part of a team, the focus is on the team, not just *you*. You are simply one part of the whole team, and it's the entire team that competes against others. To be a strong team member, you need to understand and accept your role, aiming to give your best for the benefit of the team. The most successful teams at any level are those where everyone — players, coaches, and support staff — understands and accepts their roles.

In the 1960s, Bruce Tuckman introduced a group development model called "Forming, Storming, Norming, and Performing." Teams must go through the first three stages to perform at their best. During the forming stage, there's often a tryout period, followed by moving into the locker room, and then forming the team and bringing everyone together. The storming stage can be somewhat chaotic. It's when athletes and coaches try to figure out how all the pieces fit. There can also be anxiety, as an athlete's vision of themselves sometimes differs from reality. In the norming stage, athletes and coaches become familiar with their roles, responsibilities, strategies, and other aspects. Eventually, the team reaches the performing stage, where everything starts to "click."

Learning to be a great teammate is incredibly valuable training for life. We exist in relationships with others, and whether in a work group, family, new relationship, town, or city, being a good team member enhances not only your life but also the lives of those around you.

∽

Power of Two

How Collaboration Amplifies Opportunity

We all know what a one-on-one basketball game looks like. One player faces off against another — no one else to focus on. In a one-on-one scenario, it comes down to the basics: skills, speed, size, and talent. There's no passing in one-on-one, no help defense.

When we add a second player and switch to two-on-two, notice how many things change. Suddenly, on offense, there is someone to play off of. We can pass, cut, pick, slip, roll, and move. We can fool defenders with our eyes; there's room for tact and deception. If you ever want to study this, watch how John Stockton and Karl Malone worked together for all those years in the NBA. Everyone knew a high pick-and-roll was coming, but no one consistently defended it. They created too many possibilities to defend.

As soon as another player is added, so much more opens up. It's not just about individual talent anymore. The same applies on defense — now there's help, and no one is left alone on an "island." If you get beaten, your teammate is there to help. He helps you recover. You switch on the pick, you talk. You communicate with your eyes and your voice. The court comes alive with movement and noise.

Life is like this, too. Adding even just one other person to your life can bring about profound changes. Suddenly, there's someone to play with, to share experiences with. Instead of on the basketball court, you're now playing together on life's court. New possibilities emerge as the journey is shared. It continues to grow, adding more people and making it even richer and more complex as options multiply.

Keep this in mind when you're in community with others or when that special relationship comes your way. You'll need to compromise and adapt, but remember that the whole is greater than the sum of its parts, and the outcome is much more rewarding than going it alone.

You are a social being. One plus one equals much more than two. Look for chances to collaborate, and you'll discover your best self both on and off the field. Working together makes us feel satisfied.

～

CHOREOGRAPHY AND IMPROVISATION
BALANCING STRUCTURE WITH SPONTANEITY

I learned firsthand as a coach that I couldn't expect my team to execute plays they hadn't practiced before. I tried to maximize practice time, focusing on action and movement rather than talking. It became crucial to dedicate time to both individual and team drills that would lead to top performance. I realized that coaches are like choreographers. I also found that shouting instructions to my players during the game was not very effective.

My yelling from the sideline only added noise and distraction, making it hard for players to pay attention to both me and the game. It also became clear that they couldn't rely too much on set plays — what if the opponent did something unexpected? What if the play I called out wasn't effective? Would my players know what to do next?

In my early coaching years, my players relied too heavily on me for direction during games. This became clear during a game when I had used all my timeouts, the score was tied, and my players were unsure of how to proceed. My shouted instructions weren't working, and the whole situation felt futile and frustrating. We lost that game.

So, I took a different approach. Instead of training my team to follow set instructions, I taught them to improvise, enabling them to adapt quickly to the game's constantly changing situations. Instead of focusing on a lot of set plays, we emphasized the fundamentals of both individual and team skills. Rather than giving them specific plays to run, I showed them how to be creative and how to solve the puzzles posed by their opponents. Improvisation made our teams unpredictable and hard to beat.

Life works this way, too. If you develop a core set of good values — honesty, integrity, hard work, kindness, etc. — you can then successfully adapt to our changing world in real time.

Sometimes our movement is choreographed; sometimes it's improvised. Focus on practicing the fundamentals and trust the process.

∿

CREATIVITY
FINDING FREEDOM WITHIN THE FORM

Playing sports provides clear evidence that everything is always changing. When you compete, you're placing yourself in a situation that shifts quickly from moment to moment. Whether it's the weather, the opponent, or the bounces of the ball, everything is in constant flux. Your ability to creatively adjust to these rapid changes as an athlete can be the difference between success and failure.

We can never fully predict what our opponent will try next; therefore, we must train ourselves to adapt smoothly to whatever happens. A creative athlete learns to solve problems in many ways, constantly devising new strategies to beat the opponent — or at least trying to. If you can't go through, maybe you need to go around; if not high, then perhaps low? If force doesn't work, then try deception. A creative athlete will never run out of options if their mind is open and they are willing to consider different approaches. What once seemed impossible can become completely achievable through creativity and imagination. Seen this way, creativity builds confidence.

You were born with a creative soul. Connect with your creativity through your athletic journey. This makes it more interesting, fun, and beneficial.

∼

Selflessness
Putting the Team Before Yourself

Being selfless just means recognizing you're part of a bigger whole. It involves releasing an ego that both protects and limits you. It's the realization that it's not about just *you* – it's about *us*.

When you're on a team, you contribute whatever you can for the good of the whole. The team is the whole, and you're just a part of it. The team can't succeed without everyone's dedication to the entire project. A team of selfless players is the team that has the best chance to reach its full potential. Any player lucky enough to be on a selfless team understands this feeling. It is a kind of grace experienced through giving it all to a common goal without concern for what's in it for "me."

Consider the opposite for a moment: A team of individuals who primarily care about their own personal success and statistics. These are toxic teams to be part of, where blame and selfishness replace trust and teamwork.

In life, great things are accomplished when groups of people come together and commit themselves fully to a cause. This is how families, communities, nations, and yes, teams flourish.

So, beware of your ego; it seeks gratification, recognition, and control. Instead, practice selflessness. Life presents you with endless opportunities to do this.

Give of yourself for the benefit of the group. Choose selflessness over egoism.

~

SMILE
BRINGING JOY TO THE JOURNEY

I remember a well-known Division I championship-level coach talking about his belief that players should have a smile on their face before competing. I enjoyed hearing this because it's so true. When we feel joy, we perform better. When we're happy and positive, we're more open to learning and growth.

Learn to approach your sport with joy. Yes, there will be difficulties — hard practices, losses, injuries. Yet, there is a natural joy in engaging with sports that shouldn't be suppressed. Instead, it should be shared with teammates, fans, coaches, and others. Some athletes might feel they have to be completely serious all the time. I believe you can be focused and joyful at the same time, and in fact, combining these qualities creates winners.

A smile is contagious and has a magical way of lifting your spirits and those around you. When you smile, your mindset shifts. As you read this, try a simple exercise: Stop reading and make yourself smile. What happens? Your body recognizes the smile and feels happy. You feel better. And if someone else catches a glimpse of your smile, they feel better, too!

In life, you'll face difficulties, but there's always something to be happy about. Find your happiness and hold onto it. Keep smiling.

∾

COACHING
GUIDING OTHERS WHILE CONTINUING TO LEARN

A coach must first create a *vision* for success. Specifically, what does it look like when the team or individual (in individual sports) performs at their best? This requires the coach to have a deep understanding of the sport. The coach then needs to determine how to train the team to realize that vision, making the most of practice time. Additionally, a coach must be a builder of culture and confidence, as well as an effective communicator.

A coach should be firm yet kind, recognizing the best in each player. Sometimes the coach needs to be vocal, other times, quiet. If the coach does their job well, the players will feel empowered, as if they accomplished it themselves.

Coaches are, above all, role models. When I talk with coaches and other leaders — especially team captains — I often say, "Be the way you want your team to be." Coaching isn't just about shaping others; it's about being shaped in return. The responsibility of leading people has a way of calling you forward — compelling you to grow, evolve, and expand who you are. That's part of what makes coaching such a meaningful and rewarding pursuit.

Ultimately, the coach is a helper and a guide, using sports as a way to build lasting character. Whether someone is a parent, business leader, mentor, or sports coach, coaching should be seen as an act of generosity.

A coach's job is to help people improve. To show players that they can accomplish more than they think they can. In turn, coaches grow and evolve themselves.

~

BE YOUR OWN COACH
HOLDING YOURSELF ACCOUNTABLE WITH
COMPASSION

As a young athlete, you show up at practice and do what your coach tells you to do. You wait for instructions, then do your best to carry them out. In the early stages of your athletic journey, you mainly rely on your coaches for direction. Similarly, as a child, you primarily depend on your parents. As you grow and mature as an athlete, it becomes essential to become your own coach, in a way. As your self-awareness develops, you can start to see yourself objectively — your strengths and weaknesses, what needs the most attention, and where to improve. For instance, you may realize the need to work on changing direction more effectively. Likewise, you may notice that you get anxious before games and can work on managing that as well.

Some athletes spend their entire careers simply following their coach's instructions. These athletes often fail to reach their full potential and frequently burn out during high school sports. They tend to see themselves as empty vessels into which the coach pours instructions.

They become dependable workhorses without imagination. They lack personal agency.

When you become self-aware enough as an athlete to understand what benefits you and what doesn't, you then start to become your own coach. Becoming your own coach involves recognizing the work you need to do off the practice field and taking action. It means learning to push yourself beyond your self-imposed mental limits. It means recognizing when you are being lazy and need to move into action, and when you are tired and need to rest.

When you become your own coach, you become a learner and develop the self-confidence to tackle significant challenges — whether physical or mental – independently.

Develop objective self-awareness of your strengths and weaknesses, both physical and mental. Let your inner coach drive you toward continuous improvement. Create a vision for yourself, then work to become it. Use your time wisely.

᜕

LEADERSHIP
INFLUENCE THROUGH INTEGRITY, NOT AUTHORITY

There's an old saying that "leadership is better caught than taught." This phrase suggests that by being around good leaders, mentors, and role models, you can also become a good leader. I believe in this idea and encourage athletes to observe those around them who are effective leaders. I often ask new team captains to talk about the leaders they've encountered and what qualities make someone a good leader.

Most of these athletes mention a player who may not play the most, but seems to genuinely care about everyone on the team. They describe the athlete who, despite injury, stays positive and encourages others instead of wallowing in self-pity.

I often tell emerging leaders that they need to "be the way you want the rest of the team to be." By this, I mean that if you want a team of cooperative, hardworking, and committed individuals, you must model those qualities yourself.

Humans, as social beings, tend to follow; so as a leader,

you must set the right example. Leaders in sports are athletes who tend to be present, hardworking, and inspiring to their teammates and coaches.

To become a leader, begin by studying the leadership qualities of those you respect, and then focus on developing those qualities in yourself. Leadership is shown not only through words but also through actions, but it is mainly demonstrated by actions.

COMPASSION
SEEING OTHERS CLEARLY AND WITH CARE

I would be remiss if I didn't mention the importance of compassion in this book. Compassion is empathy put into action. It's not just the desire to understand another's suffering but also the steps you take to ease it. In simple terms, it's about helping others through your actions. You might notice a teammate feels down or disconnected. What can you do actively to make that person feel included and understood? Remember, compassion isn't weak, and neither is kindness. You can be strong both physically and mentally while also being compassionate. It's one of the most vital qualities you can develop.

Being a compassionate athlete helps you understand that we all face difficulties and often need someone to know and understand us, to be there with us in our struggles.

∽

COMPETITION
Rivalry as a Mirror, Not a Measuring Stick

Today, it's common to criticize or even hate your opponent. Although this attitude might seem like a way to motivate yourself, it's flawed because it comes from negativity. I've always found this ironic, since our opponents are often just like us. They share the same passion for the sport, are roughly the same age, and care about their teammates and winning just as much as we do.

You should respect your opponent. After all, without a worthy opponent, there can be no competition. You grow and improve through regular healthy competition. It's possible to want to beat your opponent while still respecting her — you can hold these two views at the same time. You and your opponent are bringing out the best in each other.

This applies to both players and coaches. When I first started coaching, a few teams in our league consistently set the standard. Their veteran coaches built strong cultures and prepared their players with care and precision. Competing against them pushed me to raise my own game

— to become a better coach so that, one day, our teams might match theirs. Looking back, I think we all understood that the challenge was mutual — we were helping each other grow.

At the end of the day, your opponent presents the challenge, but the real competition is with yourself. Am I growing? Am I improving? What more can I work on or do to perform better? Competing against a worthy opponent helps clarify this.

Don't get caught up in negative emotions about your opponent. This not only reduces your mental focus but can also lead to a negative, contracted frame of mind and body. Keep things positive, and remember, a good opponent is what pushes you to improve.

Being a good competitor takes practice. Not giving up takes practice. Competing right through to the end of the game takes practice. Many athletes train year-round for their sport, yet they don't compete enough. The good news is that you can practice competing in other sports or activities that aren't your main sport. If you want to get better at competing, practice competing.

Embrace the benefits of competition, as it sharpens your edge. Learn to love competing as a way to discover what you are capable of. Value your opponent as someone who brings out the best in you.

~

TALK

SPEAK WITH PURPOSE, COACH THROUGH MOVEMENT

Many coaches, especially new ones, talk too much. As someone who has done this myself, I understand. Talking about the sport, the drill, the opponent, and so on can give a coach a false sense of security. "If I talk about it enough, my players will understand its importance and start doing what I ask of them." The problem with that mindset is that sports are active. Sports are about movement, often complex movements with many players.

While a coach needs to talk, great coaches know the importance of practicing the physical movements that lead to success. Talking is very different from doing, and ultimately, it's the doing that counts.

Therefore, coaches need to be self-aware enough to recognize when they start talking too much during practice. They should utilize that valuable time to allow players to train and rehearse the skills and movements that lead to success. A great coach spends a lot of time observing, and some time correcting, cajoling, praising, and criticizing.

But mainly, they focus on correcting player technique and creating practice scenarios where players can train to do everything that helps them succeed.

Sport is about doing, not talking. Coaches must remember this.

EXPECTATION
LETTING GO OF WHAT YOU THINK SHOULD HAPPEN

I once worked with a college team that believed they simply couldn't beat their arch-rival. When I asked the captains why, they said it had just become that way. Over the last four or five games, they not only lost to their rival but often lost badly.

So I asked them what it would be like if that opponent stepped onto the field with no name on their jersey? How would they play against this no-name team? And the captains replied that they'd probably play better. Why? I asked. "The pressure would be off because we wouldn't know who they are. We'd play looser and freer."

When our minds seek certainty, we form expectations based on past experiences. They realized that much of their problem was that they had convinced themselves they couldn't beat this particular team. But when they tested that belief by suddenly not knowing who they were, they were able to relax and perform at their best.

In fact, that's exactly what they did — defeating their

archrival in the conference championship game, then beating them three more times in a row.

Let go of expectations. Play the game with consistent high intensity; this honors both the game and yourself. Don't worry about the name on the jersey. Instead, focus inward and perform to your best ability.

AFTERWORD

Writing this book wasn't that hard; it was actually the easiest part of the process. I'd thought about these passages many times before finally putting them into words. As I wrote, I often heard the familiar voices of friends, family, teammates, and mentors — some departed, but never far away. Their presence and support were a quiet comfort throughout this work.

I realized that finishing this book would be the best way to share my experience and advice, and hopefully, guide others in sports and life. If a promising athlete finds this book helpful, or if it helps a coach or a parent become a better guide, that would truly make me happy.

I wanted to create something tangible and lasting. I also wanted it to be concise — something that could be read in an afternoon or enjoyed for a few minutes at a time. Something I would have appreciated when I was nineteen.

During the editing process, I thought about adding

more personal stories; however, this wasn't meant to be a memoir. The writing stirred up many vivid memories, and I realized once again how much my relationship with sports continues to shape who I am.

Peter Bidstrup, November 2025

About the Author

Peter Bidstrup has spent much of his life around sports and education. He grew up on the campus of Tabor Academy in Massachusetts, where his father, Larry, taught history and coached wrestling for 43 years. He graduated in 1986 from Franklin and Marshall College and is a member of its Hall of Fame. As a lacrosse coach, his teams won or shared 8 Independent School League titles during his 21 seasons at the Governor's Academy, where he also worked in admissions and development. Among other things, he teaches mindfulness, meditation, and performance. He has two grown children, Brett and Larsen, and a dog named Coach.